planet earth
our extraordinary world

UP CLOSE!

By Matthew Murrie and Steve Murrie

SCHOLASTIC INC.

New York   Toronto   London   Auckland   Sydney
Mexico City   New Delhi   Hong Kong

Table of Contents

Introduction

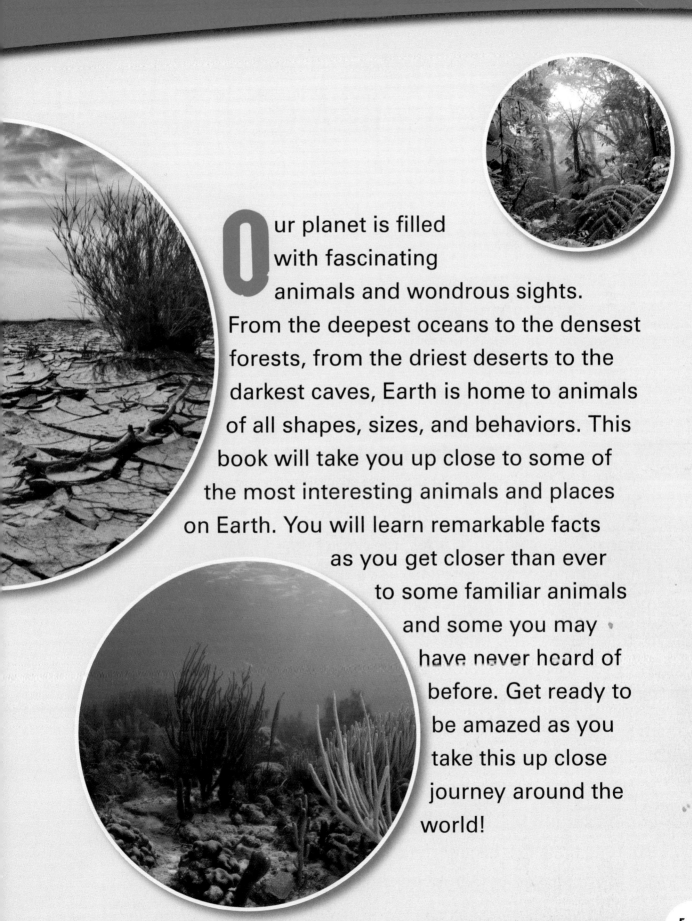

Our planet is filled with fascinating animals and wondrous sights. From the deepest oceans to the densest forests, from the driest deserts to the darkest caves, Earth is home to animals of all shapes, sizes, and behaviors. This book will take you up close to some of the most interesting animals and places on Earth. You will learn remarkable facts as you get closer than ever to some familiar animals and some you may have never heard of before. Get ready to be amazed as you take this up close journey around the world!

Ocean Deep

Octopus Arms

What sea animal has a soft body, 8 arms, and lives on the ocean floor? An octopus, of course! While octopuses are best known for their 8 arms, it is what they can do with their arms that makes these sea creatures truly bizarre. Octopuses are able to taste their food with the suction cups that dot each of their arms. And they can detach an arm on purpose. Why? Because after it is detached, it still wiggles, which attracts predators while the octopus makes a quick getaway.

Octopuses are also masters of camouflage. The mimic octopus, for instance, is capable of changing its shape and coloration to make it resemble other, more dangerous sea creatures such as an eel, sea snake, or lionfish.

And when camouflage does not work, these elusive critters spray a black ink in the face of their pursuers. Not only does this ink interfere with a predator's vision, it is also believed to disrupt its sense of smell.

Jellyfish Head

What animal's head is full of jelly but has no brain? That is a "no brainer" — it is a jellyfish. The jellyfish is one of the oldest living creatures in the world. They have existed on this planet for over 650 million years. The "jelly" in a jellyfish is a thick elastic substance that gives this sea animal its shape as well as its name.

Jellyfish are dangerous because the venom they release from their tentacles can be excruciatingly painful. The sting of some jellyfish may pack more than just intense pain. The venom of the box jellyfish is believed to be the most poisonous on Earth.

The jellyfish's body also helps this floating animal stand up against its predators. Thanks to the transparency of the "jelly," they can go undetected by potential predators. If they are not careful, predators can get caught in a jellyfish's tentacles and transform from predator to prey in an instant.

DID YOU KNOW?

The ideal water temperature for the vampire squid is a chilly 35 degrees Fahrenheit (1.7 degrees Celsius). *Brrrr!*

Vampire Squid Eye

Despite its name, the vampire squid is more closely related to an octopus than a squid. These deep sea animals can be found in oceans throughout the world. While most vampires are known for the size of their teeth, the vampire squid is known for the size of its eyes. Proportionately, they have the largest eye-to-body ratio of any animal. Not only are their eyes about as large as human eyes, but with a diameter of about 1 inch, their eyes make up nearly 10 percent of their 12 inch (30 cm) bodies. If a human were to have the same proportions, our eyes would be as large as our faces.

Why are their eyes so big? Since vampire squids live more than 3,000 feet (914 m) below the ocean surface, they need extra large eyes in order to see through the darkness. When squids detect a potential predator, they distract the predator by releasing a cloud of sticky mucus full of glowing blue balls.

Shallow Seas

Brain Coral Tentacles

The brain coral has learned the secret to longevity — they can live for up to 200 years! And they understand the importance of community — several of these small corals can form a colony over 6 feet (1.8 m) tall! Brain coral, like all corals, are made up of the skeletons of tiny sea creatures. They can be found in shallow, warm-water coral reefs in all the world's oceans. During the daytime, brain coral may not appear any more active than a rock on the ocean floor, but there is something living and breathing beneath the coral's surface.

Perhaps the most important part of the brain coral are their tentacles. During the day, these tiny arms are pulled in close to their bodies for protection. At night their tentacles shoot out to catch food. Some corals even use their stinging tentacles to fight against other brain corals.

DID YOU KNOW?

Brain coral can withstand strong storms that break other types of coral. They use their tentacles to tightly grip their surroundings.

Dugong Snout

Although often referred to as "sea cows," dugongs are actually related to elephants. In fact, these large marine mammals, which can be found swimming in warm coastal waters from East Africa to Australia, even have ivory tusks jutting out from the sides of their mouths. Males use these tusks to fight other males, and females use them to protect their young from predators. Their long powerful snouts are similar to an elephant's trunk; however, instead of grabbing peanuts, dugongs use their snouts to vacuum up seagrass from the ocean floor.

Dugongs may appear pretty laid-back, but they have serious appetites. One dugong can devour a bed of seagrass the size of a soccer field in one day! Sailors exploring the coastal shores in the tropics once mistook Dugongs for mermaids off in the distance.

The name *dugong* may mean "lady of the sea," but the animals are commonly referred to as "sea cow" or "sea pig."

DID YOU KNOW?

Despite all of those sharp teeth, great white sharks do not chew their food. Try chewing a piece of food with just your front teeth. Not an easy task!

Great White Shark Teeth

The great white shark is the largest predatory fish in the ocean. They can grow to an average length of 15 feet (4.6 m). Great whites are keen hunters. Their mouths are lined with up to 300 sharp teeth, arranged in several rows. It is not surprising that there are so many shark teeth to be found, since sharks lose as many as 30,000 teeth in their lifetime.

Sharks lose their teeth easily because their teeth are not connected to their jaws. Instead, these sharp teeth sit in a shark's gums while replacement teeth constantly grow and wait below their gums. Most sharks have 2-3 rows of teeth with 20-30 teeth in each row. The whale shark has 300 rows of tiny teeth!

Sea Star Stomachs

Sea stars are spiny, hard-skinned animals that live on the rocky sea floor. They may appear to be innocent, passive creatures but sea stars are actually merciless predators. In fact, they are capable of devouring prey much larger than their mouths. What is their secret? They have two stomachs!

One of the sea star's stomachs digests food, while its secondary stomach extends out from its body to eat prey. Sea stars use their arms to pry open the shell of food such as a clam. Then they squeeze their second stomachs into the opening. Once inside the shell, the stomach goes to work devouring the clam from the inside. When it is full, the sea star pulls back its stomach and lets go of the empty shell.

What if the clam clamps down on one of the sea star's arms? No worries, it will grow a new one! In fact, even if 4 of its 5 arms are lost, a sea star can regenerate to a full star.

DID YOU KNOW?

A young queen angelfish will set up a cleaning station and pick parasites off the skin of larger fish such as hammerhead sharks and mantas.

Queen Angelfish Skin

The queen angelfish is one of the most attractive reef fish. They get their names from the ringed spots on their foreheads that look like a queen's crown. This lovely fish has a sparkling blue and yellow body with a rounded head. Their top fins, or dorsal fins, run the entire length of their bodies and they have solid yellow tails. When mature, the queen angelfish can reach up to 18 inches (45 cm) long and can weigh up to 3.5 pounds (1.6 kg).

Queen angelfish live in and around the coral reefs that stretch from Bermuda to Central America and onward to Brazil. Unlike most fish, queen angelfish are usually found in pairs. It is believed that these pairs stay together for life. The female can lay 25,000-75,000 eggs at one time; and as many as 10 million eggs during one breeding season.

Freshwater

Nile Crocodile Scales

The Nile crocodile is the largest species of crocodile living in Africa. These endangered animals can be found in rivers, freshwater marshes, and mangrove swamps throughout sub-Saharan Africa, the Nile Basin, and Madagascar. Their skin is rough, scaly, and waterproof — perfect for protection in the water and the sun. Their backs and tails are covered with rows of scaly knobs.

The Nile crocodile measures in at more than 16 feet (5 m) long and weighs over 500 pounds (225 kg). Incredibly, these massive crocodiles can flatten themselves to hide in water that is only 12 inches (30 cm) deep in order to sneak up on their prey.

Crocodiles might look clumsy on land, but they sprint faster than most humans. In the blink of an eye, crocodiles can go from sitting still to running 8.5 miles (13.68 km) per hour!

DID YOU KNOW?

Sometimes, crocodiles will run so fast they lift the front portion of their bodies off the ground.

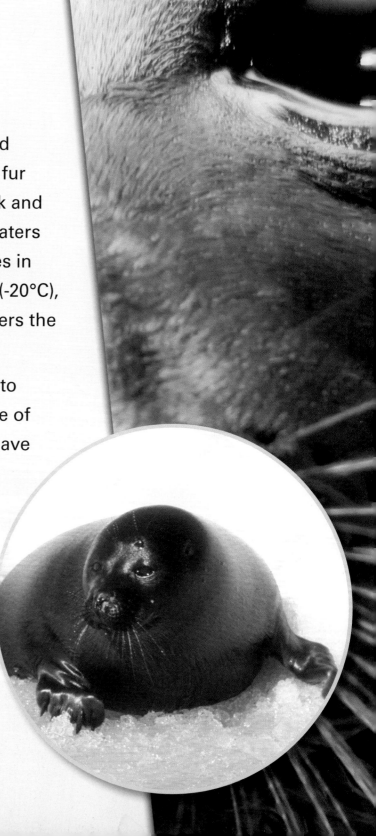

Baikal Seal Fur

The Baikal seal can be found in and around Lake Baikal in Siberia. The fur of a Baikal seal has to be very thick and dense to keep it warm in the icy waters of Lake Baikal. Winter temperatures in this region of Russia average -4°F (-20°C), and nearly 4 feet (1.2 m) of ice covers the lake from January to March.

The Baikal is only 4 to 4.6 feet (1.2 to 1.4 m) long, which makes them one of the smallest types of seals. They have the remarkable ability to remain underwater for as long as 70 minutes and can dive as deep as 935 feet (300 m), which is 3 times the length of a football field! Baikals feed on the translucent golomyanka fish, which live in the deepest part of the lake.

Baikal seals can live for more than 50 years.

Rainforests

Bullet Ant Spikes

Lowland rainforests are the home to millions and millions of insects, including the reddish-black bullet ant. Bullet ants are one of the world's largest ant species, measuring up to an inch (2.54 cm) long. If you look closely at a bullet ant, you may see a head full of spikes. These spikes are actually growths produced by parasitic fungus. The fungus will grow the spikes using body tissues and fluid found inside the ant. The spikes will produce thousands of spores that can then infect other bullet ants.

If a bullet ant is discovered acting strangely, other ants will know it is due to the fungus infection. The infected ant will be carried away from the colony so it will not infect the entire colony.

This parasitic fungus is very selective and will infect only bullet ants. There is good news though — parasitic fungi keep insect populations from overpopulating the rainforest.

DID YOU KNOW?

Bullet ants get their name from the pain their bite inflicts, which is often compared to the feeling of being shot with a bullet.

Emperor Tamarin Moustache

The small, active emperor tamarin monkey lives in the dense Amazon rainforest. Both the male and female emperor tamarin monkeys have moustaches. While scientists are not certain as to the purpose of this monkey's moustache, it certainly is astounding to see such a large moustache on such a small animal. Emperor tamarins also have amazing tails, which are longer than their bodies.

Emperor tamarins eat fruit that they find high in the branches of trees. These agile monkeys climb onto tiny branches and grab fruit that larger monkeys cannot reach.

Here's something else that is fascinating about the emperor tamarins — the males take care of the babies. They have even been known to take care of baby monkeys that do not belong to them.

DID YOU KNOW?

The male emperor tamarin can only see two colors and females can see three.

DID YOU KNOW?

A hummingbird will collect nectar from as many as 1000 flowers per day.

Hummingbird Tongue

The hummingbird is the only bird that can fly backwards, and that's not all — they can also fly forwards, sideways, and even upside down! Their tiny wings beat up to 80 times a second, causing a humming sound — hence their name.

Hummingbirds also have a special split tongue that is designed to feed on the nectar of flowers such as the azalea and honeysuckle. Hummingbirds use their tongues to lick nectar at the rate of 13 times a second. Their tongues are about as long as their bills, which average between 0.6 to 0.8 inches (15 to 20 mm).

Hummingbirds are called nectivores because 90 percent of their diet is flower nectar. However, they will catch flying insects in mid-flight for an occasional snack. The hummingbird can digest a fruit fly in less than 10 minutes. This is important because the extra weight in their stomachs would require more energy to fly.

Gliding Leaf Frog Webbed Hands

Can you imagine using your hands and feet as parachutes? The gliding leaf frog is one of the many species of tree frogs that can be found living in the tropical rainforests of Colombia, Costa Rica, Ecuador, and Panama. They use their extensively webbed feet to glide from branch to branch in the rainforest. Gliding tree frogs can glide horizontally up to 13 feet (4 m)!

Baby gliding leaf frogs begin their lives high up in the trees. The female will deposit between 14 and 60 eggs on the upper surface of tree leaves high above a stream or pool of water. When the eggs hatch, the tadpoles fall down into the water below and grow into froglets. After a few months, the froglets crawl out of the water and scale up a nearby tree — to the canopy where they spend the rest of their lives.

DID YOU KNOW?

There are over 630 different kinds of tree frogs.

Rainforests

DID YOU KNOW?

Jaguars are different from other big cats in that they like water and are very good swimmers.

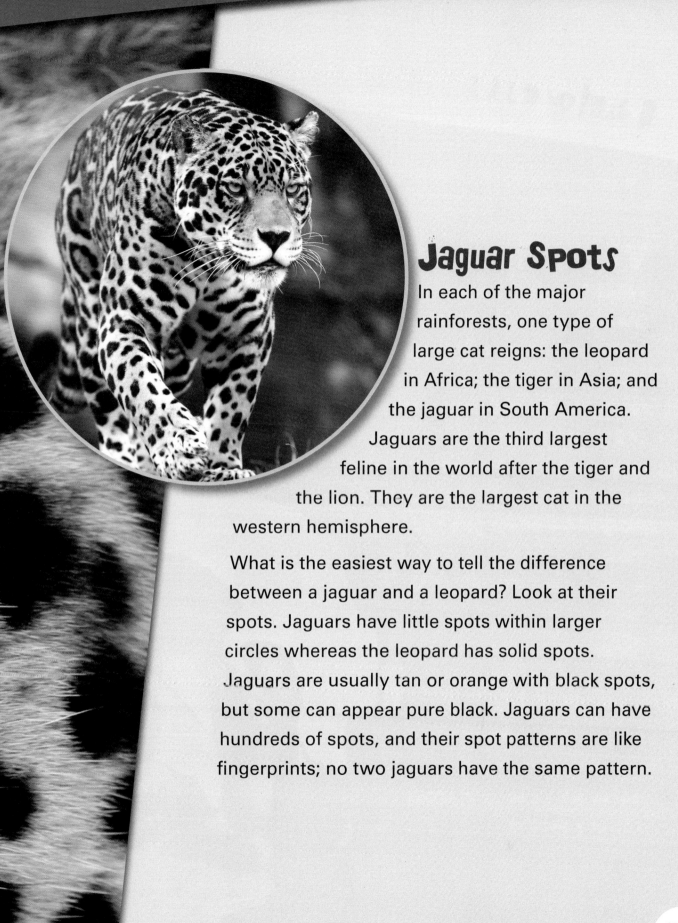

Jaguar Spots

In each of the major rainforests, one type of large cat reigns: the leopard in Africa; the tiger in Asia; and the jaguar in South America. Jaguars are the third largest feline in the world after the tiger and the lion. They are the largest cat in the western hemisphere.

What is the easiest way to tell the difference between a jaguar and a leopard? Look at their spots. Jaguars have little spots within larger circles whereas the leopard has solid spots. Jaguars are usually tan or orange with black spots, but some can appear pure black. Jaguars can have hundreds of spots, and their spot patterns are like fingerprints; no two jaguars have the same pattern.

Venus Flytrap Hairs

Venus flytraps are one of the planet's few carnivorous plants, feeding on insects and spiders. These fascinating plants, found only in a small section of North and South Carolina, eat about 1 or 2 insects in a month. They normally take about 5 to 12 days to completely digest their catch. If a rock or other indigestible object gets trapped inside a venus flytrap, the plant will spit it out after about 12 hours.

Those may look like tiny hairs on a venus flytrap, but they are actually triggers. If something hits 1 or more of the hairs, the leaves will close up in about 1/10 of a second.

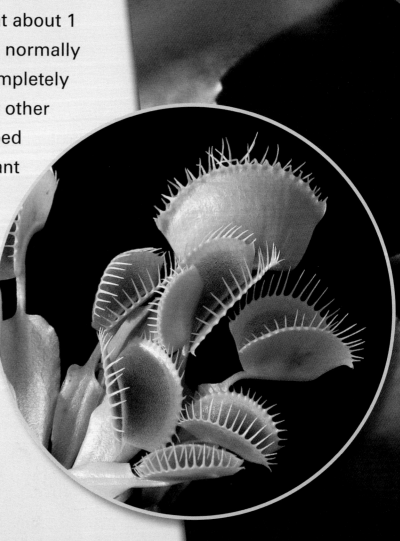

DID YOU KNOW?

The venus flytrap can survive wildfires.

Great Plains

Dung Beetle Legs

Nature has its own, specialized cleanup crew to take care of the dung (feces) that is dropped by grazing animals in Africa — dung beetles. Right after dung has hit the ground, male dung beetles arrive to do their job. They use their back legs to roll the dung into round balls. Then they present these stinking balls to female dung beetles who lay their eggs in them.

After laying a single egg, the female buries the dung balls as deep as 3 feet (about 1 m) in the ground. When the eggs hatch into larvae, they feed on the undigested food in the dung. The part that is not eaten is used to fertilize the soil, which helps to grow more plants, which get eaten by animals that produce dung and the cycle goes on and on. In the Serengeti plains, three quarters of all dung is recycled by the dung beetles.

One type of dung beetle in South Africa has been known to ride on the back of a large snail that produces dung for the beetle.

Asian Elephant Skin

Whether from Africa or Asia, the elephant is the largest land mammal in the world. The Asian elephant is slightly smaller than its African relative and can be found in the plains, savannahs, and jungles of India and Southeast Asia. All elephants have thick skin that helps them stay cool. Their gray or brownish color allows them to blend into their shady environments. Asian elephant skin is less wrinkly than that of the African elephant.

Male Asian elephants have visible tusks, while females may only have small tusks that are located inside their mouths. Wide, padded feet help them walk quietly through the jungle. And their large, flappable ears help these huge animals cool off — unless of course there is water nearby. All elephants love to cool off in the water.

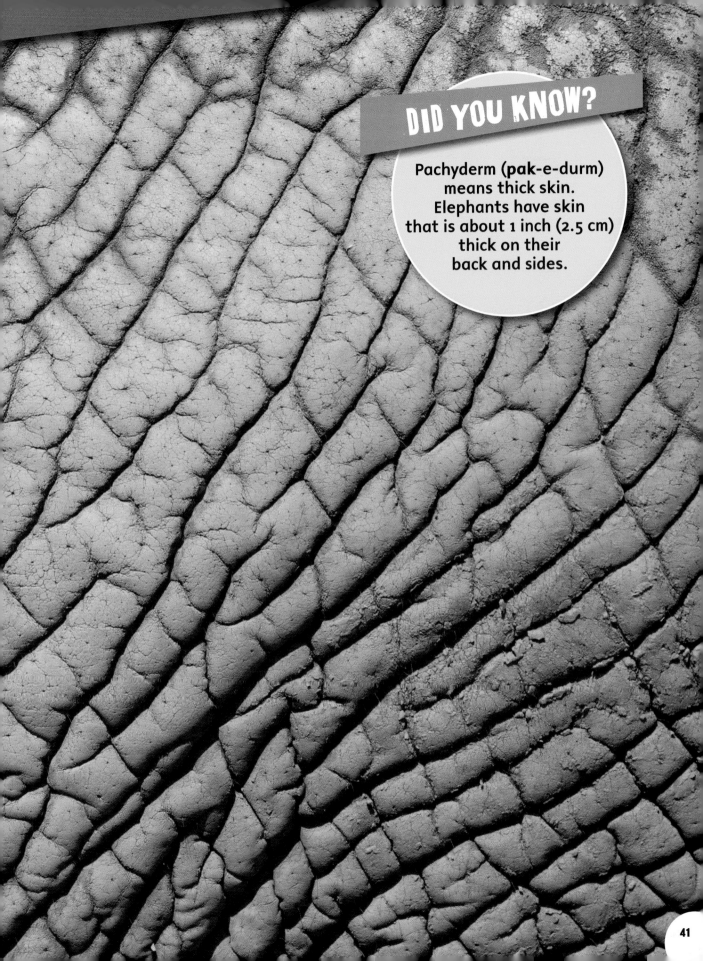

DID YOU KNOW?

Pachyderm (pak-e-durm) means thick skin. Elephants have skin that is about 1 inch (2.5 cm) thick on their back and sides.

DID YOU KNOW?

In Alaska, there are twice as many caribou as people!

Caribou Antlers

Closely related to the reindeer, the caribou is a large North American member of the deer family. A caribou's antlers are made of a type of bone that grows quicker than any other bone. This is a good thing for caribou, since they lose and regrow their antlers every year. And boy, do those bones grow! Caribou antlers reach lengths of up to 3 feet (0.9 m) and can have more than 40 sharp points! Caribou happen to be the only members of the deer family in which both the male and female grow antlers.

Caribou also travel more than any other land animal on the planet. Every year, they wander over 3,000 miles (4,828 km). That is more than the distance between Maine and California! Why don't they just stay put? They get hungry. Since plants do not grow much in the cold tundra, they must keep moving to find enough food. Once they eat all of the available plants in an area, it is time to move on.

Forests

Capercaillie Tails

The capercaillie, found across northern Europe and Asia, is the largest member of the grouse family. This eccentric bird seems to love attention. The striking white markings, set against the dark, bluish-green background on the male's tail feathers, are used to attract the less colorful females.

The male capercaillies have another way of getting noticed. They begin each morning by singing. After a few notes, they jump to the ground and begin dancing to their songs. While dancing, they fan out their tails and point their beaks in the air.

This melodic bird can create an orchestra of sounds including drumrolls, popping corks, tapping, and gurgling. The capercaillies' singing is so powerful that their songs can be heard miles away, but not by humans. Much of these large bird's songs are sung out of the range of human ears.

DID YOU KNOW?

It doesn't happen often, but when two male capercaillies fight, they sometimes do so to the death.

Forests

DID YOU KNOW?

The word moose comes from the Algonquin word "mooswa," which means twig eater.

Moose Hooves

The moose, the world's largest deer, is most recognizable by its unique antlers. The males, or bull moose, shed their antlers every year in the late autumn and grow new sets each spring. These enormous antlers are used to scare off predators, but their hooves are the moose's first line of defense. Moose are very strong kickers and will use their hooves to defend themselves. Their hooves also help them get away fast — moose can run up to 35 miles (56.33 km) per hour.

Moose live in the northern forests of North America, Europe, and Russia. The cold weather does not slow them down. Their hooves act as snowshoes, supporting them on soft snow or frozen marshes. Moose are also terrific swimmers. They can swim for miles at a time.

Cicada Wings

The insect known as the periodical cicada has one of nature's most unusual life cycles. The female cicada cuts tiny openings into the bark of tree branches and lays her eggs. The eggs then hatch into larvae that travel to the ground and burrow into the soil. They plunge their needlelike mouthparts into the roots of the tree and remain underground for 17 years, living on the tree sap.

In the spring of the 17th year, they dig out of the ground, climb the tree, and find a leafy branch to begin their metamorphosis into adults. The adults emerge from their shells as white and soft, but after just two hours they have hard exoskeletons.

Male cicadas begin making a loud screeching noise. After hearing the males' calls, females will flip their wings quickly, creating a sound that can range from a soft rustle to a sharp crack.

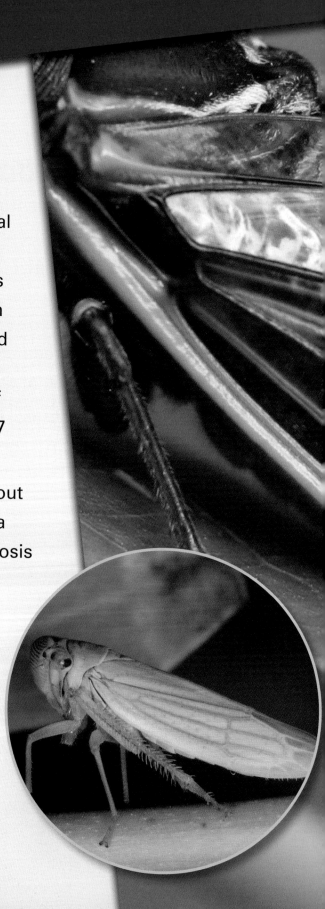

DID YOU KNOW?

Have you ever heard the screech of cicadas on a summer evening? Some cicadas are so loud they can be heard up to 1 mile (1.5 km) away.

Deserts & Open Savannas

Dromedary Camel Eyelashes

One hump or two? The dromedary camel distinguishes itself from other camels by its single hump. But did you also know that all camels have three eyelids? That's right, this desert dweller's trio of eyelids is just another way the camel copes with the harsh conditions of its desert home. The Sahara Desert's sandstorms can reach up to one mile high (1.6 km) and can be several miles wide. A camel's top two eyelids have eyelashes while the bottom one is very thin with no eyelashes. Camels also have extra-long eyelashes — 4 inches (10 cm), which helps to keep the sand out of their eyes.

And that's not all — they even have long, hair-filled nostrils that can be closed one at a time in order to keep sand from flying up their noses.

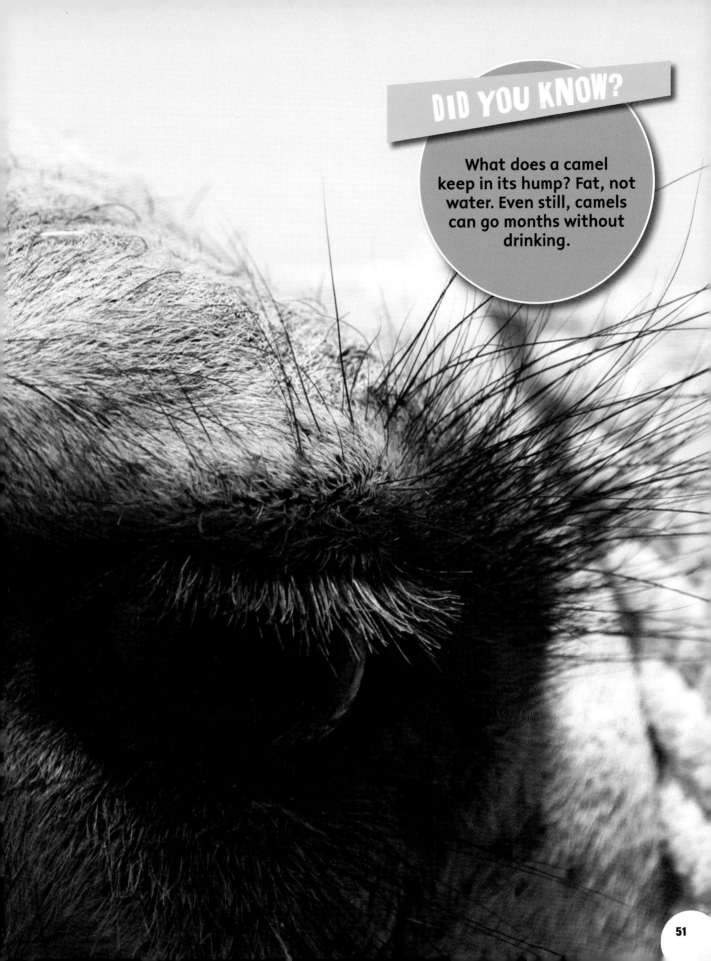

What does a camel keep in its hump? Fat, not water. Even still, camels can go months without drinking.

African Lion Mane

Fiercely protective of his pride, or family group, the male lion patrols a large area in the open African savanna. While it was once believed that the function of a lion's mane was to protect its neck when fighting, it is now believed that the primary purpose of a lion's mane is to attract females. The longer and darker the mane, the more mature and attractive the lion appears to a lioness.

The majestic mane may also look like a crown, but lions are not, nor ever have been "kings of the jungle." Why? Because they do not live in jungles. In fact, lions can live in just about every habitat *except* jungles. While they prefer to live in open woodlands and savannas, they can also be found in deserts and plains.

DID YOU KNOW?

A lion's mane, while attractive, can cause him to overheat.

DID YOU KNOW?

The female gaboon viper gives birth to live babies — as many as 50 at a time!

Gaboon Viper Venom

Native to central Africa, the dangerous gaboon viper has the largest snake fangs in the world at 2 inches (5.08 cm) long. Yet, believe it or not, these snakes are not *poisonous*. Confused?

Actually, it is their venom that is poisonous. Snakes are *venomous*, which means they inject venom into their victims. When examined closely, one can see that a snake's fangs are actually hollow. Those fangs are connected to venom glands that are similar to the glands that produce saliva in humans.

Snakes have voluntary control over the amount of venom they release in a bite. They can even "dry bite," in which no venom is injected. The venom in bites can range from a single drop to several fluid ounces, depending on the size and mood of the snake.

Augrabies Flat Lizard Skin

Is it a boy or a girl? Take another look. If you can see the lizard, it is probably a male, since they have bright, rainbow colors covering their bodies. Females, however, are dull brown in color in order to camouflage them against the rocks on which they spend most of their time. Why are the males so colorful? They use their intensely brilliant coloration to attract females for mating and to settle territorial disputes.

These lizards, also known as the Broadley's flat lizard, live in the rocky areas of the Augrabies Falls in South Africa. Where does the "flat" part of this lizard's name come from? It comes from the lizard's ability to squash its body flat so it can fit into small places — like the cracks of a rock.

DID YOU KNOW?

The augrabies flat lizard can do a 360 degree backflip to catch flying insects.

DID YOU KNOW?

Zebras are naturally attracted to black and white stripes. Given the chance, they will walk over to stand next to a black-and-white-striped wall.

Burchell's Zebra Stripes

Just like snowflakes and human fingerprints, every zebra has a unique stripe pattern. Do the black and white stripes help camouflage the zebra? The answer is yes . . . sort of.

A zebra's main predator, the lion, is color-blind, and can get confused by a large group of striped zebras. When zebras are running, their moving stripes break up their outlines, making it difficult for a lion to strike a single animal. The stripes even distort distance at dawn and dusk.

Of the three species of zebras, the Burchell's zebra is the most widespread. Also known as the common or plains zebra, they live in large herds in the Serengeti plains of Africa. Zebras can run up to 35 mph (56 kph). Newborns can walk after only 20 minutes and run after just one hour. Foals, or baby zebras, are born dark brown and white instead of black and white.

Frozen Poles

Emperor Penguin Collar

What could be cuter than a group of penguins huddled together for warmth in icy Antarctica? When baby emperor penguins hatch, they are covered with warm down feathers. After one year, young emperor penguins develop a yellow collar. As they age, this collar will darken to a deep orange. The emperor penguin has the highest feather density of any bird, with roughly 100 feathers packed tightly into every square inch (6.5 square cm). They need all of those feathers to keep their skin dry while swimming in the icy Antarctic Ocean.

These penguins also find warmth in numbers. The males gather together in a large group called a colony. Colonies of emperor penguins have been found with as many as 40,000 birds huddled together in a close circle. During this time, the males have a special job; they keep an egg, laid by a female, warm until it is ready to hatch.

DID YOU KNOW?

Emperor penguins
never live on dry land —
they spend their time
in the ocean or on an
ice shelf with
the ocean
underneath it.

Polar Bear Feet

What's colder than a polar bear's toenails? Not much. A polar bear's feet and claws are quite different from the feet of other bears. While their claws are shorter and stubbier, their feet are much larger. A polar bear's foot can be as large as 12 inches (30 cm) wide. These short claws and wide feet make it easier for polar bears to live in their arctic environment.

Having a larger foot surface to maintain their heavy weight, polar bears are able to keep stable footing on snow and ice. Their wide feet also serve as flippers, making them remarkable swimmers.

And those claws? Not only are they short, they are shaped like tiny scoops, which help the polar bear dig winter homes in the snow.

DID YOU KNOW?

Polar bears' fur may look white but it is actually clear. Their fur is made of hollow tubes which absorb sunlight.

Frozen Poles

DID YOU KNOW?

An adult walrus has about 6 inches (15 cm) of blubber underneath its skin.

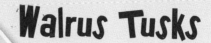

Walrus Tusks

Long-tusked walrus are most often found near the Arctic Circle, lying on the ice. These marine mammals are extremely sociable and can be heard bellowing and snorting to one another.

Walruses use their tusks to obtain food and to fight for social dominance. Tusks also come in handy for pulling their immense bodies out of the water.

Perhaps even more remarkable than their tusks, are their whiskers. There are between 400-700 whiskers on a walrus's snout. Those whiskers can grow to about a foot (30 cm) long, but are usually worn down as walruses also use their whiskers to find food and sweep it into their mouths.

Not only are their whiskers strong enough to dig for clams, they are sensitive enough to distinguish the differences in shapes as small as a pebble. And walruses make their whiskers work hard. An adult walrus can eat 6,000 clams in a single meal!

Caves

Lechuguilla Cave Crystals

Discovered in 1986, the Lechuguilla (le-**choo**-gee-uh) Cave is considered to be one of the most beautifully decorated caves in the world. The cave has many rooms and passages, including the chandelier room, which has 20 foot long (6 m) chandeliers made of pure white gypsum crystals. Since gypsum is a very soft mineral, touching the crystals could damage them.

It is no wonder that the cave is off limits to tourists. In fact, its exact location is a closely guarded secret and only a few scientists and professionals are allowed to enter the cave. Unlike most caves, Lechuguilla was formed from the bottom up instead of the top down. Hydrogen sulfide gas bubbled up from the Earth's crust and then mixed with oxygen and formed sulfuric acid that dissolved the rocks and formed the cave.

Stalactites/ Stalagmites

Stalactites (stuh-**lak**-tites) are solid mineral deposits that hang down from the ceilings of caves. Every stalactite begins as one drop of water full of dissolved minerals. The drop falls from the ceiling and a very small amount of solid mineral remains on the ceiling. Stalagmites (stuh-**lag**-mites) are the same but form on the floor of the cave. When a stalactite and stalagmite join together, a column is formed.

Stalactites grow very slowly — 0.005 inches (0.13 mm) a year. It takes a century for most stalactites to grow from a quarter of an inch to one inch. The fastest ones have been observed growing 0.12 inches (3 mm) a year, or about the same thickness as two pennies. The longest stalactite is reported to be found in Lebanon's Jeita Grotto with a length of 25 feet (8 m).

DID YOU KNOW?

A way to remember the difference between a stalactite and a stalagmite is this: Stalactites have to hold tight (tite) to the ceiling so they don't fall off!

DID YOU KNOW?

Three million wrinkle-lipped bats can be found living in just one cave in Borneo, an island in Southeast Asia.

Wrinkle-Lipped Bat Lips

Bats are the only mammal that can fly. And they are very skilled at what they do. A single cave colony of wrinkle-lipped bats catches 4 tons of insects on their nightly flights. Many of the insects are mosquitoes that spread diseases. About 70 percent of all bats feed on insects. Many tropical bats feed entirely on fruit and nectar while a few are carnivorous and feed on fish, frogs, mice, and birds. The wrinkle-lipped bat's lips help direct sound waves to their ears when they are using echolocation to identify food and objects in their flight paths.

When they return to the cave, they attach to the ceiling and when they poop it drops to the cave floor. These droppings are called *guano* and are used by farmers to fertilize their fields. Scientists have found mounds of guano piled into balls as high as a 15-story building.

How can bats hang upside down all night? Bats have specialized tendons in their toes that allow them to cling to the cave ceiling without straining their muscles at all.

Belizean White Crab Mouth

The unique Belizean white crab spends its life in dark caves in and around Central America. Venturing out from their rocky dwellings in search of food could prove deadly if they were to cross the path of a predator. So these crabs have learned to make do with devouring whatever falls their way — including bat guano. Considering what else is available to eat in a cave, bat guano is one of the richest sources of nutrients for these crabs.

Why can't these crabs see? Since they live their entire lives in underground waterways, Belizean white crabs live in a world without light, so eyes would be totally useless.

DID YOU KNOW?

Animals like the Belizean white crab that spend their entire lives in caves, are called troglobites (**trog-lo-bytes**).

Monal Pheasant Neck

The monal pheasant lives in the high latitudes of the Himalayan Mountains and nearby regions of Afghanistan, Bhutan, Pakistan, and Western China. Monal pheasant must dig for their food. Instead of using their feet like some birds, monal pheasants use their beaks to dig in the ground. They have been known to dig a hole about 7 inches (18 cm) deep looking for tubers, insects, and other foods.

Male monal pheasants wear feathers of flashy, metallic blues, greens, red, and purple for others to see, while females tend to dress down in dull brown and black. The most colorful part of the females' appearance is the distinctive blue ring around their eyes. When the male monal pheasant hatches, its neck plumage resembles that of the female. It takes about a year before its feathers transform into the bright colors of the flashy, adult male.

ts

The monal pheasant is the national bird of Nepal.

Snow Leopard Spots

The snow leopards' 100 or so black spots sprinkled across their heavy white and gray coat help camouflage them in the rocky mountain terrain. Living in the high, rugged mountains of central Asia, snow leopards use their camouflage effectively to sneak up on their prey. They are excellent hunters, with the ability to capture animals 3 times their size.

The bigger the kill, the quicker the leopard must get it back to its den. The mountains are full of scavengers such as wolves and vultures who will gladly eat the leopard's dinner. And they can forget about scaring off these unwanted dinner guests — unlike other big cats, such as the lion or tiger, the snow leopard cannot roar.

DID YOU KNOW?

The snow leopard can jump the length of a school bus — with over 3 feet to spare!

Conclusion

Our world is filled with incredible things and there is always more to see. The closer you get, the more you learn about the remarkable Planet Earth.

OUR WORLD, OUR HOME

From frozen poles to humid rainforests, our extraordinary world is full of astonishing discoveries. The best part is that there's still more to learn about the world around us! But unfortunately, many of these natural wonders are in danger. Habitats are threatened and many animals hover near extinction. We all live on Planet Earth, and it is important to keep learning about the world around us, and to support conservation efforts. See the list below to learn about some things you can do to keep our planet healthy.

- **Bring Your Own Bag.** If you're going shopping, bring your own reusable bags with you. Plastic bags are made from petroleum (aka oil) and paper bags are made from trees. So if you bring your own bag, you won't be wasting either!

- **Don't Leave the Fridge Open.** Try to decide what you want before you open the fridge or freezer door — that way all the cold air won't escape.

- **Down the Tubes.** Turn off the faucet when you're brushing your teeth! You'll save lots of water from going down the drain.

- **Line Dry Your Laundry.** Hang your laundry on an old-fashioned clothesline instead of using an energy-guzzling dryer. You will save lots of energy and you'll lower your parents' electric bill, too!

- **Unplug It.** Unplug all your chargers when you're not using them. Chargers suck up energy even when you're not charging anything, so by pulling the plug, you'll be saving energy.

- **Just Say No to Plastic Water Bottles.** Instead of using disposable plastic water bottles, get a reusable container to bring water with you. Tossing out plastic water bottles creates a huge amount of waste.

- **Reusable Containers Rule.** When it comes to your lunch, the less packaging, the better. Individually wrapped snacks and drinks waste resources. Instead, use reusable containers from home to bring your food to and from school.

- **Ban Styrofoam Products.** Styrofoam never decomposes, making it an environmentally unfriendly choice. Instead of using disposable Styrofoam products, use reusable ones. The Earth will thank you.

- **Put Your Computer to Sleep.** Using a screensaver on your computer uses more energy than if you let it go to sleep. So change the preferences on your computer and give it a rest.

- **Watch Out for E-Waste.** E-waste, or discarded cell phones and computers, is a growing problem. Keep electronics for as long as possible and dispose of them responsibly. You can find an organization that will donate your old electronics to be refurbished.

- **Remember the Three R's.** Reduce. Reuse. Recycle. These are important ways to cut down on consumption and waste.